Pleasure Track, watercolor, oil and charcoal
on paper, board, canvas, 48 ½″ x 60″, 1995.

Soft as Cotton, Centered and Hard

PAINTING AND POETRY

Franklin
WILLIAMS

Library of Congress Catalog Card Number: 97-69029

ISBN: 0-9659655-0-3

The book "Soft as Cotton, Centered and Hard"
with paintings and poetry of Franklin Williams
was published in November 1997
by Stoá Gallery and Publishing,
Petaluma, California
fax: (707) 778-6222
web site: www.stoa.com

Design: Ion Frantzeskakis, Ionic Concepts, Petaluma, California
Printing: Paris Printing, Inc., Novato, California

Introduction

by Stuart E. Williams

For most, it may be impossible to fathom that the majority of times it is the less obvi-
ous circumstances that surround us in our everyday life that lead to a greater understanding, yet for myself it is true. As a child I would often visit my father at work, and
I can distinctly recall the sheer fascination I carried for exploring the many different
casts and molds he and a handful of his students would leave behind as waste.
Although as a result of my childhood curiosity I was introduced to these primarily fig-
urative molds or casts at a young age, it was not until some years later that I became
enlightened enough to realize what they truly were.

Through my father's profession, he has been blessed with the opportunity to not
solely develop as an individual, but to help show those who have developed the correct sense of being, a path on which they too can reach a contentedness in their heart.
Franklin Williams has done for a lifetime what all of us have wanted to, yet none of us
seem to; that is to primarily live a life free of the societal handcuffs worn by you and
I. His paintings are the medium he has chosen to give others a spiritual snapshot into
his mind, soul, and heart. Together with his poetry, one can correlate the message and
attempt to develop an even more vivid understanding of not only the artist, but themselves as well. Combined, these two means of expression form a solid unit into which
one may begin to explore their own personal fantasies and/or demons. That is to say,
not all of what we view or feel in art is pleasurable, it is not. In life, as well as in his

Franklin Williams in his Studio

art, not all that interact with my father are going to walk away from a confrontation with him or his works with a condition of supreme well-being. A permanent impact will undoubtedly occur, and should the result be either positive or negative, perhaps one should take it upon themselves to explore the deepest conclusion of why. One cannot be afraid of straying from what they know and are in comforts with if they are to fully understand what lays ahead throughout these pages.

While the majority of us methodically march along through life and follow what those who surround us prescribe as correct; you may then rest assured that should you chose to travel through this wonderful adventure of self-sacrament, a personal enlightenment is a true possibility. That same enlightenment that occurred when I realized that those leftover molds and casts that I once marveled as a child only mirrored those that today constantly try to contain me. My father has spent his entire life free from the molds and casts of society and has romantically as well as painstakingly attempted to share that possibility with both his students and those dear to his heart. While apparently a number of his students did break free and leave those molds behind to stimulate the curiosity of a child, unfortunately many others have carried them into their lives forever. Whether it be through his class, family, art, or this book, my father has constantly and will forever express himself to those who are willing and capable to not merely listen, but ascertain what is said.

PROFILE

My head is tilted, showing the
power of my profile,
I stand alone, upon a yellow pine floor,
hands extended.
Seeing myself as a young boy,
rainbows of colored love, cover
by body.
Charged with passion, legs
parted, I gaze at the paintings
hanging on the wall.
Body rhythms paint the
jewel of passing time.
Light moves across the yellow
pine floor.
My body edged with a thousand
lines of moving love.
Through line mind of elegance, I continue to
invest within my
erotic form.

MARRIED

Yes, I am married to a dream princess.
Her calls, full of my echoes of required dreams.
Dream princess, within her world,
existing on such a high stage,
stars and gods, stand in silence of her beauty.

I have experienced her view,
her landscapes, her inner space.
Traveling I arrive at a place of
amazement where I have never been.

She made me form myself from
the inside out, all other voices are
alien, hostile, I call for her goodness, and love.

I tell myself she is not beyond my comprehension,
dream princess, given to my heart,
keeping my soul so solitary, and safe.

I am so true to my devotion,
enormous powers dwell inside,
teaching without limits,
doing my best to be patient
with the divine, of my inspiration.

Absorption, oil and charcoal on paper and wood, 77 ½″ x 84½″, 1995.

TEACHING

Following the father in tradition of
imagination, revelation, wisdom and romance,
I am immersed in thoughts of love.
I know a man woman boy girl child
desperately holding a flickering light.
Crushed by criticism, have we forgotten the love of youth?
Painting a test of strength,
I move dark shelled devils of criticism
to passion and imagination of emotion and mood.
Teaching them
to live in trust of being, to desire,
invent, to reflect in the secrets they contain.
Learning singular faith in tenderness and time,
for art is a strange revelation,
knowing nothing of criticism,
every day teaching trusting, not knowing where I am going.

Muddy Knees, oil and charcoal on wood and paper, 76″ diam., 1996.

I STAND ALONE

Four frames of sun light,
warm.
Four white walls,
a studio.
A chamber of love,
a sacred place, where three
paintings hang in a line of red.
My body alight with the anticipation,
of the light of my mind.
I stand alone, I raise my hands,
ten colors of circular dots.
Decorative, patterned painting,
delicately rendered.
My line moves once again, helping to define
the uncertainty of the figures trapped red,
in line.

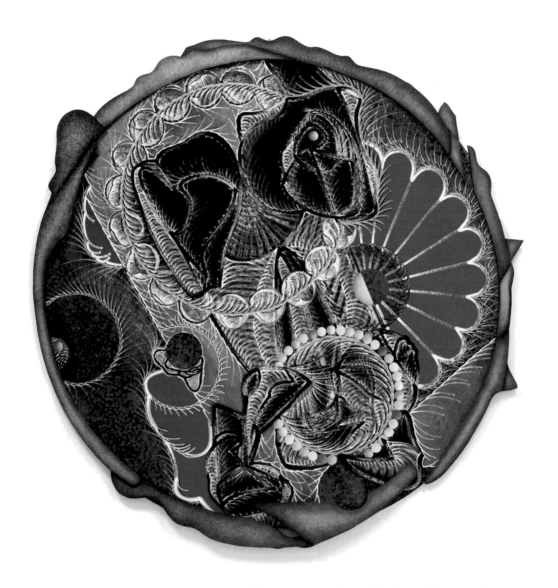

I Stand Alone, oil and charcoal on paper and wood, 65″ x 65″, 1996.

WHO

My eyes
they see enormous things
so private
a hint
a silence
Who hears my voice?

I can not stop asking who hears, hears, hears,
Who hears my voice?
My voice becoming quiet within the greatness
of my gift.

Working in the presence of angels,
looking in wonder, waking, walking,
in my gifted garden.
Who hears, hears, hears, who?

Private Hint, oil and charcoal on paper and wood, 45″ diam., 1994.

WORK

To make art is to sing with the human voice,
the voice I need is the voice I already have,
revealing the light of my mind through the
ordinary work of my art,
engaging the issues that matter to me,
getting on with my work,
with only my self to fall back on,
I consistently keep after it,
through a sense of certainty.

Working Voice, oil and charcoal on wood and paper, 67″ x 58″ x 13″, 1993.

VOYEUR

I seem to be living, am I awake? Is it all pretend?
Within my circular, squared triangle,
I am moving round and round.

At times I feel as a voyeur,
I lay on flat colored human form.
Upon their surface, wet and dry,
cool and hot, I touch them with my
lines of beloved color.

Watching as the voyeur,
it is easy to feel my love for some,
my hate for others,
I move,
pushing myself to angles of maximum visibility.

There is a softness, a hardness,
to the angles of circular fantasy.
Her figure continues to gently pull my brush
around and around, so not to disturb my vision.
Finding myself so impatient, so eager,
I continue round and round with marked delight.
At times so awake, or is it all pretend?
Does it matter?
Round and round
I move.

Power Rings, oil and charcoal on wood and paper, 76″ x 76″, 1996.

MOOD CERTAIN

Hiding nothing I feel my own
tender personal gesture.
Putting myself in the delight of life
twisted and turned,
with hard understanding of
patterned dreams, decorative vision.
Mood certain
I pull lines from vines
carefully defined.
Moving smooth eloquent silence
I live in the middle of my mind,
uncovering my body mysteries
bowl of perfume.

A Glimpse, oil and charcoal on wood and paper, 48 ½″ x 60″, 1995.

GREATER

I, greater than my parts,
parts beyond ideas, rhythms and metaphors.
Unable to analyze time and logic,
I plunge into a flood of associations,
erupting into images of excess,
fine and beautiful,
coming naturally as nature.
I, recorder of visions, laboring to
the center of self,
creator, stimulator, preserver
and up holder of my talented organ
of sight.

Body Edged, oil and charcoal on wood and paper, 68″ x 68″, 1997.

COSMIC DUDE

Yes
Cosmic Dude,
the Press told me so.
The room inside is light and dark.
Yes
I am a man room of self taught fashion,
full of laws, vast and orderly.
Yes
Systematic.
Yes
a man room with eyes,
fashioned and self taught.

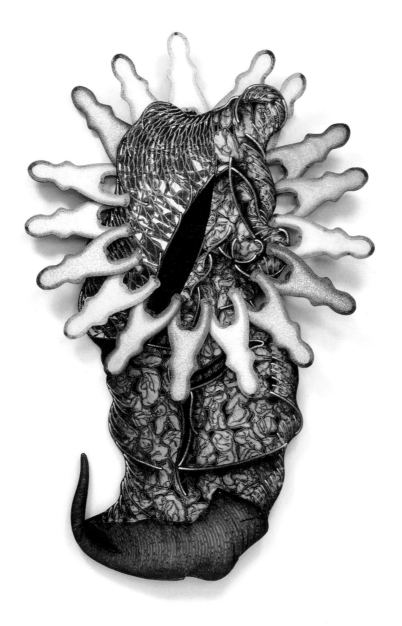

Cosmic Dude, oil and charcoal on paper and wood, 50″ x 76″, 1995.

MOMENTARY SEIZURE

Three graces dance in a circle,
beauty, restraint and pleasure,
the graces of my life.
Desire shoots her flaming arrow at restraint.
The arrow of desire and attachment,
stop me in my tracks.
I am taken by beauty, and feel her pleasure.
Momentary seizure feeds my soul
with its preferred diet of light,
sight, inviting contemplation.
Beauty's source of imagination, never dries up.
Soul seized,
individually, I display my arrested heart.

Circular Seizure, oil and charcoal on paper and wood, 70″ diam., 1996.

Aching, oil on paper, 17″ x 21″, 1994.

ACHING

I reach to touch, finding
only my body aching, old
elegant hands, feathered
red with grace, margin
touching, gently remembering,
echoes of childhood, tenderly
loved, bursting in bloom,
body aching, alone I linger.

Male Traveler, oil on paper, 17″ x 21″, 1994.

BEAUTY IS BORN

Within my child, purest essence,
following bent inspired divine
visions of imagination.
I nervously move curves of beloved
celtic bounding lines.
Travelling male,
belonging to timeless time,
my beauty is born.

Image, oil on paper, 17″ x 21″, 1994.

IMAGE

A feeling of fullness, opens my mind,
mixing my day with the closing of time.
Opening and closing my eyes, images fly,
hand to hand, father and mother die, who
lives on my path of love but my wife,
followed by sons and brides,
sources of life, love sappy.

Cupped Torso, oil on paper, 17″ x 21″, 1994.

DRUNK

Enlightened with the madness of my manhood,
I drink endlessly from my personal cup,
full of strange streaks of self insanity.
Floating,
full of trial and error,
groping, stumbling, questioning, looking,
never finishing,
I am with self,
enthusiastically drunk.

Privacy, oil on paper, 17″ x 21″, 1994.

PRIVACY

There is no possibility of my privacy being invaded.
Within my uncommon studio chamber,
I squeeze nature power from pigment.
Rings of red light bathe my figure.
With a posture of ease,
I raise my hands to touch,
line upon line, yielding artifacts,
within twisted twine.

Question, oil on paper, 17" x 21", 1994.

QUESTION

Do not question,
simple signs of living vision,
touched alive within my dreams.
Slowly, slowly, rooted,
peaceful working within.
Simple sign,
sexual obsession,
do not question.

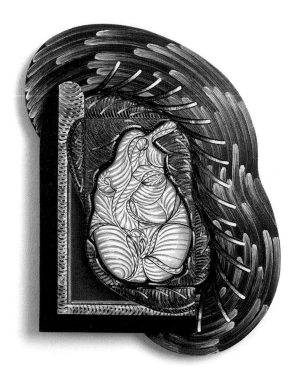

Fine Spun, oil on wood and paper, 13 1/2″ x 16 3/4″, 1994.

KISSED BY BEAUTY

Alone in my dreams,
feeling my fire of madness,
reckless passion, weakened by age,
bring back my youth as a naked lover,
fine spun, but not fragile.
Kissed by beauty,
I plunge into excesses of sex,
in a fire of silence and madness.

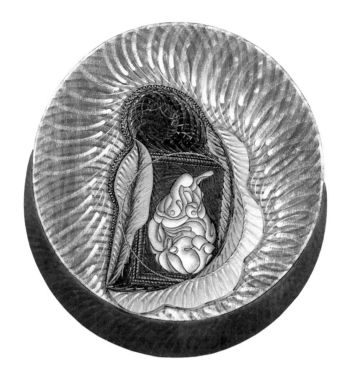

Not Me, oil on wood and paper, 25 ½″ x 27 ½″, 1993.

LAUGHARNE

In my understanding of my misunderstanding,
there is a quiet lonely sound in my heart,
for this moving soundless place,
Laugharne.
My heart, a quiet room of fantasy.
God's sunny face defined in the outline of my body,
with blue forget-me-nots,
my soul.
Oh God,
I seem so alone,
in all my understanding of my misunderstanding.

LOOKING

I answer with a smile of love
eyes of wisdom stir my brain.
Standing before a looking glass
with the pleasure of knowing line,
edged bright, clear and sharp,
my body is drawn.
Jetting myself to memories,
I plunge through hot touched thoughts.

Body Drawn, oil, watercolor and charcoal on paper, 38″ x 50″, 1991.

MOVING

Looking at a stick covered with hair,
black lines move gracefully
upon the ground of brown.
Black birds screeching,
a moment of unexpected hope.
Brushes move wet smooth oil
across my feelings,
pushing human fragments to the surface.
Floating torso, a glimpse, a breast,
a search for balance.
Dancing figures edged with black velvet lines,
cling to the joy of the moment.
Pushing, pulling, pale veils of gray.
Looking at a stick covered with hair,
moving feelings, moving.

Black Birds, acrylic and charcoal on paper, 38″ x 50″, 1991.

LINE TIME

Following the passionate, linear, loving,
linked line.
Clear and determined.

Knowing my beginnings,
I travel away from man's style and manner.

With the love of the human,
I search for self nourishment,
Greek matters.

Lost in my demon,
following the passionate, linear, loving,
linked line,
I move my time.

Line Time, acrylic and charcoal on paper, 38″ x 50″, 1990.

FINDING MYSELF CONTAINED

In language are echoes of what
I have said. Pressed in clay, longing,
I say longing, for approval of
original clay. Back remembering
forward looking, the clay at times
seems so blurred and empty.
Why am I hiding?
I squeeze the clay and look away
within. Within they seem to be
unable to see source moving
sounds of love. It seems so far
away, fed with tastes of wet warm
clay, squeezing source sounds
each and every day.

Echoes, acrylic and charcoal on paper, 38″ x 50″, 1992.

Flowering Bloom, acrylic and charcoal on paper, 38″ x 50″, 1990.

I

Accepting my good luck, I cry
out loud, and weep, crying out, do
not be silent, have no fear. I must
light the darkness and desolate
sights, I must live within my self
a hope, I must frame with the
light of my mind, quickly and
quietly, pictures of understanding.
I must draw sticks of gray
feelings, forms flowering in
bloom, centered and torn.

Orange Twilight, acrylic on canvas, 60″ x 60″, 1983.

TWILIGHT

I saw her face today.
Twilight, starlight, eyelight,
gentle deep and gray.

I saw her face today.
Lips sweet, gently speaking,
chanting ever, ever, evermore, alone.

I saw her face today.

OLD MAN SING

Sing, sing, song,
old man sing,
beautiful song.
Mournful song, sung,
sing separation, exile, death.
Old man sing,
sing of love sweet.
Old man sing,
heart in shadow song.
Lovers melt in twilight song
old emotional form.
Fall silent old man,
sing, sing, song.

Dad's Stone, acrylic on wood and canvas, 32 ½″ x 80″ x 5″, 1982.

EAGERNESS

Waiting on my wobbling star, moon facing,
fragments of adorned figures awaiting,
given to my edge, star colors mix my emotions,
I turn my head.
Viewing rainbow light, white, blue and
red, eager finger prints bend lines
of light, close and far, shifted and bent.
Old and waiting, years of listening,
stars dust my mind.
Figures form power rings of light,
ticking flashes of insight.
Facial star, wobbling expression, quiet life,
slow withdrawal.

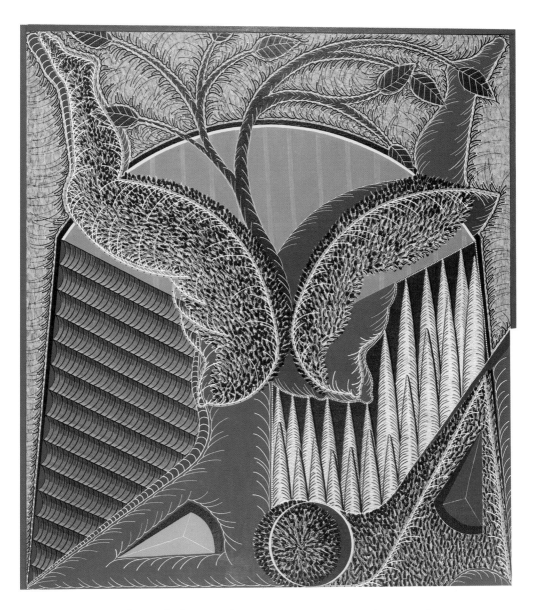

Ticking Flashes, acrylic on canvas, 55 ½″ x 62″, 1986.

ELEGANT

Eye acts of devotion move wet sweet
lines of oil to a still center of my
painting. In memory of a simple
but elegant wetness, red surrounds my
figure cut from the square of
discreet suggestions. Oval shapes
repeat again and again, brilliant
in blue, shine shadow of sun.
I can't explain the devotion
living sweet in the end of my brush line,
searching further away,
than here.

Sun Cave, acrylic on canvas, 55 ½″ x 62″, 1982.

SECRET CRY

With movement and suddenness
I view a glimpse of the early and divine.
In inspiration and innocent play,
comes startling beauty, forming her
appearance within indefinable
shapes, visible and narrow.
Her wave rhythms stir wonderful
remembering of jerky beginnings.

Melancholy, a substance of beauty.

Lines take shape
flickering in her bare torso,
weighty white breasts,
light sound color,
long energies evoke emotions.
Looking useless and feeble
I give myself to my love,
shaped with line sound and color,
revealing my clinging power.

Times Arrow, acrylic on canvas, 72″ x 72″, 1978.

GAZE

I see her beauty five feet wide,
six feet tall,
soft as cotton within her center,
hard as oak on her edges.
I turn to look,
I am tantalized by the exceeding beauty,
red, yellow and green,
white lines define beauty's shape,
scattered with early, morning light.
Wet from my bath I hide in the
comfort of my green chair, worn with time,
I see her as if for the first time,
I become transfixed.
Beauty seems so still within her measurements
she is so unaware of my eyes admiring her beauty.
I gaze until I am in my center,
all ravishing forms fade,
only remembering my hands moving.
Aroused with passion, I paint,
the wet soft cotton of two figures,
separate but in love.

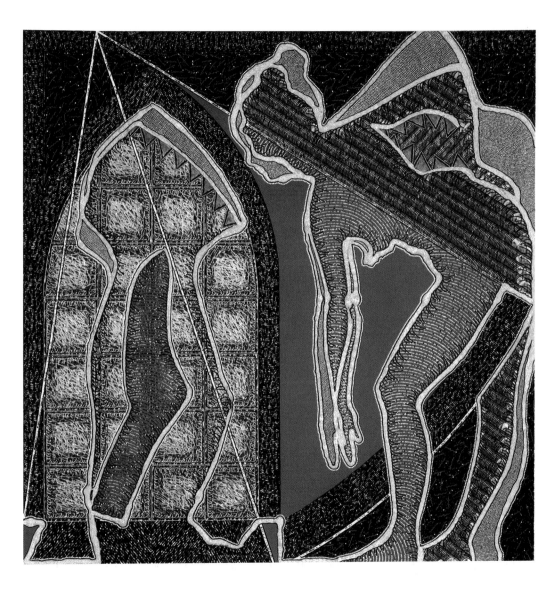

Spine-Orbit Relations, acrylic on canvas, 72″ x 72″, 1978.

SWEET

In my lush garden green full
and elegant, shade painted sweet.
Patterned brilliant colors appear,
sweet cool and full. Eyes trained,
timed sweet with repetition, looking
in amazement sweet figure
slowly appears. Stitched blue with
line pulled across the sweet pink
of flesh. Paying attention knowing
sweet separation from figure.
Small detail, I work simply
sweetly, peacefully in isolation.
Passing form, catching sweet, sweet,
beauty, staring.

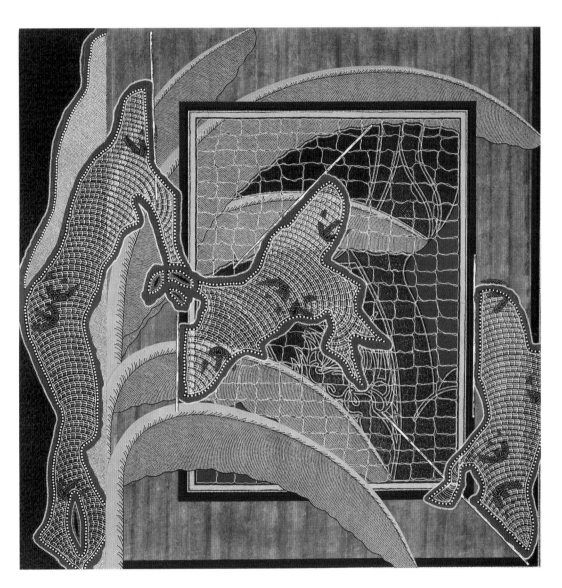

Lust and Affections, acrylic on canvas, 72″ x 72″, 1978.

MALE MAVERICK

Live maverick man as an
unbranded range animal.
Do not accept the accepted patterns,
man maverick.
Divert from the circular path,
go on, try.
Set your axis off center,
live maverick,
live singular and male.

Male Maverick, acrylic, twine, fabric on canvas, 40″ x 48″, 1972.

PUSH

Pushed by Ruth to the light of day,
I move in the work world of the master,
Ogden born.
Ruelon pushed swirling male rhythms
pressed in passion.
Sturdy form, erotic eruption shaped by my nature,
I am dazzled by visions.
Ruth and Ruelon interpreted the moment.
Ruth sings,
I listen,
full of love's fire,
singing, seize, seize, seize opportunity.
Quickly leap, leap up, reach up, hang on, on, hang
on alone, on your form,
hang from your ceiling,
caught in your storm.
Act, seed, protest, protect your
little boy man in and out,
protect, hang, hang on.

Ruth Sings, acrylic, twine, fabric on canvas, 48″ x 40″, 1973.

SELF

Try to explain
try to present yourself to your self.
Are you self - I
torment - I
perhaps play.
Do not cave into man's lowest
plateau of collectivism.
Self discover - I mysterious
inner world.
Emerge within your individual phenomenon.
Battle for the higher - I – self - I.

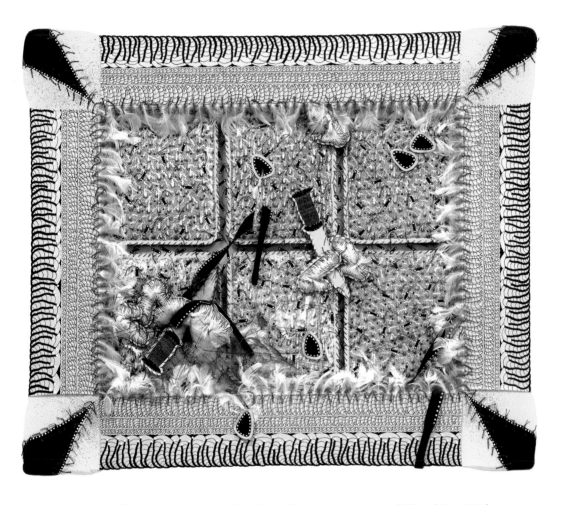

Self Stuffed, acrylic, twine, feathers, fabric on canvas, 48″ x 40″, 1974.

TALKING

Seeing in two, in and out voice of color,
reflecting eyes looking out, what is your
intension while tracing my cup, ringed
red, with blood? Angels form, still as the
night, sun pours to the ground, breaking
dots of light, freshening sight, I have to
go back to the black of the night, I
must not sleep while viewing the
sight, warm as the sun, touched,
inside, I sit in the dark caught
talking to God, death will take me
away soon enough, a knock, not yet,
come back blind as birth, in love.

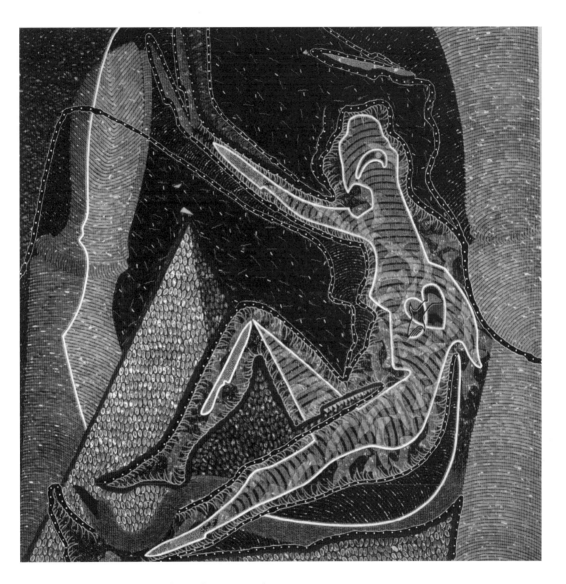

Vision of Darkness, acrylic on canvas, 72″ x 72″, 1978.

SEPARATION

Oh how sweet the feeling of
separation from the group, of the
dull stupefying boredom of the
social tittle tattle.
I live so truly in the corner of
my secret, sacred garden, away
from their extremely unsociable
surroundings of self serving certainty.
I have been cut out as with a pair
of scissors, sharp and clear, from
the massing of the unlovable
herd, to be more and more alone
in my loveable garden.

Cutting Apron Strings, acrylic and twine on canvas, 5'x 5', 1982.

GLOSSY

Those colors evoke memories of my past.
The making of a little box,
painted full of female figures.
Devotion to color,
I pattern flat glossy beauties,
Celebrating the love of the female body.
Visions of past images evoke memories,
of my elegant youth.
Little box,
big box
expand my vision,
of glossy beauties.

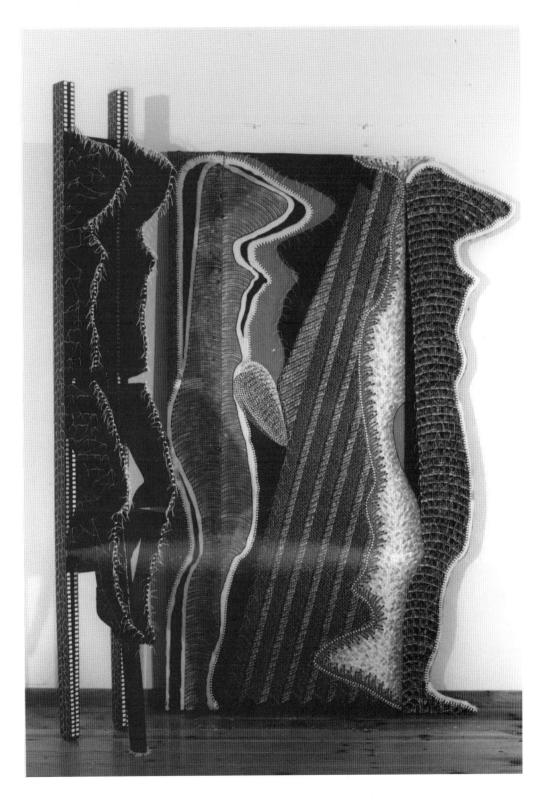

Glossy, acrylic, yarn, twine, 5' x 6' x 18″, 1980.

MATTER

Fragments fall upon my page,
white as a skeleton twisted and
turning, possessed with magical power.
Scissors cut a remarkable figure
from my circle surface turning.
A layer of tight white skin
pours across my figure.
In larger life, angels seem to inform,
giving attention to the
smallest fragments, of matter.

Matter, acrylic, yarn, canvas, 15″ x 20″ x 15″, 1966.

POSTURE

Unreached by the sea or sky I do not
hear the grown and moan of a
bitter life. Guarding the earth,
with the love of my mud, bird
chirping, color popping, I feel as a
hermit easy and out. Muddy knees
in ritual prayer pull in,
there is no sacrifice.
Visions push to my chest, touching objects
undefined, body learned, I travel,
gardening with God in the kneeling
posture of time.

Posture, acrylic, yarn, canvas, 22″ x 36″ x 15″, 1966.

PORTRAIT

Dream framed dreams,
portrait man, self framed radical Christian.

Dream framed dreams,
mother taught school of loving passion.

Dream framed dreams,
married child like elegant girl, mother.

Dream framed dreams,
portrait eccentric, undeniable,
reckless dreamer.

Dream framed dreams,
outrageous, extravagant, imaginative man.

Dream, framed, dreams
irregular love man of madness.
Dream, framed dreams,
dream, dream, dream,
dream.

Untitled, acrylic, yarn, canvas, 16″ x 12″ x 12″, 1966.

FRANKLIN WILLIAMS

Born in Ogden, Utah, Franklin Williams lives and works in Petaluma, just north of San Francisco.

Education
1958-1960	Carbon College Price, Utah
1960-1964	California College of Arts and Crafts, BFA
1964-1966	California College of Arts and Crafts, MFA

Scholastic Honors and Awards
1964	Utah Pallet Club	Painting Award
1965-1966	California College of Arts and Crafts	Spencer Mackey Scholarship
1966	California College of Arts and Crafts	MFA with Honors
1966	Ford Foundation	Painting and Sculpture Grant
1968	Lytton Center of Visual Arts	Painting and Sculpture Award
1968	National Endowment for the Arts	Painting and Sculpture Grant
1993-1994	Who's Who in American Art	Listing

Teaching
1966-present	San Francisco Art Institute (1980-1981, Chair)
1969-present	California College of Arts and Crafts
1968	University of California, Davis
1967	California State University, Hayward
1990	Ruskin School of Drawing and Painting, Oxford, England
1990	Gwent College of Higher Education, Newport, Wales

Visiting Artist
1978	Chicago Art Institute, Chicago, Ill.
1978	Charles Stewart Mott College, Flint, Mich.
1988	AICA, New York City Studio

Solo Exhibitions

1959	Carbon College, Price, Utah
1964	New Mission Gallery, San Francisco, Calif.
1966	Motion Gallery, San Jose, Calif.
	Richmond Art Center, Richmond, Calif.
1967	Yuba City College, Yuba City, Calif.
	Dilexi Gallery, San Francisco, Calif.
	California College of Arts and Crafts Gallery, Oakland, Calif.
1968	Crocker Art Museum, Sacramento, Calif.
1969	Phyllis B. Kind Gallery, Chicago, Ill.
	Arleigh Gallery, San Francisco, Calif.
1970	Davis Art Center, Davis, Calif.
	University of California, Davis, Calif.
1971	Quay Gallery, San Francisco, Calif.
	Zoecon, Palo Alto, Calif.
1972	Gallery Mark, Washington, D.C.
	St. Mary's College, Moraga, Calif.
1973	Gallery B, Paris, France
	Quay Gallery, San Francisco, Calif.
1975	Braunstein/Quay Gallery, San Francisco, Calif.
1976	Braunstein/Quay Gallery, San Francisco, Calif.
1977	Gallery K, Washington, D.C.
	Braunstein/Quay Gallery, San Francisco, Calif.
1978	Diablo Valley College, Pleasant Hill, Calif.
	Charles Stewart Mott Community College, Flint, Michigan
1979	Braunstein Gallery, San Francisco, Calif.
1980	Braunstein Gallery, San Francisco, Calif.
	Gallery K, Washington, D.C.
	Sheppard Fine Arts Gallery, University of Nevada, Reno
1981	Braunstein Gallery, San Francisco, Calif.
	Sonoma State University Gallery, Rohnert Park, Calif.
1982	Braunstein Gallery, San Francisco, Calif.
1983	San Jose Museum of Art, San Jose, Calif.
	Gallery K, Washington, D.C.
	Braunstein Gallery, San Francisco, Calif.
1984	Utah Museum of Fine Arts, Salt Lake City, Utah
	Arkansas Museum of Art, Little Rock, Arkansas
1985	Braunstein Gallery, San Francisco, Calif.
1987	Braunstein Gallery, San Francisco, Calif.
1988	AIC Fine Arts, Los Angeles, Calif.
1989	Braunstein Gallery, San Francisco, Calif.
1990	University of the Pacific, Stockton, Calif.
	Ruskin School, Oxford, England
	Somerville School, Oxford England
	Branson School, Ross, Calif.
1991	American River College Gallery, Sacramento, Calif.
	Mattei's, Petaluma, Calif.
1992	University of the Pacific, Stockton, Calif.
1993	Joseph Chowning Gallery, San Francisco, Calif.

1995	Studio Gallery 713, Petaluma, Calif.
	L. Noel Harvey Gallery II, Santa Fe, New Mexico
1997	Stoá Gallery, Petaluma, Calif.
	Nora Eccles Harrison Museum of Art, Logan, Utah

Juried Group Exhibitions

1963	Jack London Square Art Festival, Oakland, Calif.
	Richmond Art Center Annual, Richmond, Calif.
	Outdoor Art Fair, Lytton Savings, Oakland, Calif.
1964	Lithographs by Bay Area Artists, San Francisco, Calif.

Curated Group Exhibitions

1963	Some New Art in the Bay Area, San Francisco Art Institute
1964	A Collection Representing 57 Years, Oakland Art Museum, Oakland, Calif.
	Six Painters, New Mission Gallery, San Francisco, Calif.
	Southern Oregon College, Ashland, Oregon
1965	Richmond Art Center, Richmond, Calif.
	Art Indoors, Berkeley Gallery, Berkeley, Calif.
1966	San Jose Junior College, San Jose, Calif.
	California College of Arts and Crafts Gallery, Oakland, Calif.
	15th Annual, Richmond Art Center, Richmond, Calif.
	Portland Art Museum, Portland, Oregon
	Seattle Art Museum, Seattle, Washington
1967	Dilexi Gallery, San Francisco, Calif.
	Funk Art Show, University of California, Berkeley, Calif.
	30th Anniversary Exhibition, Richmond, Calif.
	Funk Art Show, Institute of Contemporary Art, Boston, Mass.
	San Jose Art Center, San Jose, Calif.
	Artists' Contemporary Gallery, Sacramento, Calif.
	1967 Painting Annual, Whitney Museum, New York, New York
1968	Sally Judd Gallery, Portland, Oregon
	University of Oregon Art Museum, Portland, Oregon
	Galleria Odyssia, New York, New York
	University of California, Davis, Calif.
	1968 Sculpture Annual, Whitney Museum, New York, New York
	San Francisco Museum of Modern Art, San Francisco, Calif.
	Northern Illinois University, DeKalb, Ill.
1969	Esther Robles Gallery, Los Angeles, Calif.
1970	San Francisco Art Institute, San Francisco, Calif.
	Drawing Invitational, San Francisco Art Institute, San Francisco, Calif.
	Richmond Art Center, Richmond, Calif.
	DeForest, Schlotzhour, Williams, Arleigh Gallery, San Francisco, Calif.
	Gallery Marc, Washington, D.C.
	College of Marin, Kentfield, Calif.
1971	New Zealand Museum, Auckland, New Zealand
	Govett-Brewster Art Gallery, New Plymouth, New Zealand
	Quay Gallery, San Francisco, Calif.
1972	Nut Art Exhibit, California State, Hayward, Calif.
	Quay Gallery, San Francisco, Calif.

	National Museum of American Art, Washington, D.C.
1973	Quay Gallery, San Francisco, Calif.
	Statements, Oakland Museum, Oakland, Calif.
	Quay Gallery Group Show, Pomona College, Pomona, Calif.
	Contemporary Arts, Washington, D.C.
	San Francisco Art Institute, San Francisco, Calif.
1974	San Francisco Art Institute, San Francisco, Calif.
	University of Nevada, Las Vegas, Nevada
1975	San Francisco Art Institute, San Francisco, Calif.
	Oakland Museum, Oakland, Calif.
	Phyllis Kind Gallery, Chicago, Ill.
	Braunstein/Quay Gallery, San Francisco, Calif.
	139 Spring Street, New York, New York
	Hansen Fuller Pays Tribute to the S. F. Art Institute, San Francisco, Calif.
1976	Whitman College, Walla Walla, Washington
	Central Washington State College, Ellensburg, Washington
	Pullman Museum of Art, Pullman, Washington
	Braunstein/Quay Gallery, San Francisco, Calif.
1977	Bay Area Artists, Oakland Museum, Oakland, Calif.
	Braunstein/Quay Gallery, San Francisco, Calif.
1978	Braunstein/Quay Gallery, San Francisco, Calif.
	Isabell Percy West Gallery, Oakland, Calif.
1979	Braunstein/Quay Gallery, San Francisco, Calif.
	Major Works, Gallery K, Washington, D.C.
1981	Abstractions, San Francisco Art Institute, San Francisco, Calif.
	Surface Design/The New Decorative, San Jose State University, San Jose, Calif.
1982	Richmond Art Center, Richmond, Calif.
	Diablo Valley College, Pleasant Hill, Calif.
1983	On and Off the Wall, Oakland Museum, Oakland, Calif.
1984	Dilexi Years (1958-1970), Oakland Museum, Oakland, Calif.
	San Francisco Bay Area Painting, San Francisco, Calif.
	Sheldon Memorial Art Gallery, Lincoln, Nebraska
	Boise Gallery of Art, Boise, Idaho
	Center of Fine Arts, Miami, Florida
	Jacksonville Art Museum, Jacksonville, Florida
1985	Laguna Beach Museum of Art, Laguna Beach, Calif.
1987	Isabel Percy West Gallery, Oakland, Calif.
1988	IAC Fine Arts, Laguna Beach, Calif.
	Emanuel Walter/Atholl McBean Gallery, San Francisco, Calif.
1992	Emanuel Walter/Atholl McBean Gallery, San Francisco, Calif.
	Modernism, Santa Monica Civic Center, Santa Monica, Calif.
	Joseph Chowning Gallery, San Francisco, Calif.
1993	Joseph Chowning Gallery, San Francisco, Calif.
1995	Joseph Chowning Gallery, San Francisco, Calif.
	Emanuel Walter/Atholl McBean Gallery, San Francisco, Calif.
1996	Past, Present, Future, Oliver Art Center, Oakland, Calif.

Select Public Collections
Oakland Art Museum, Oakland, Calif.
University of California Berkeley Museum, Berkeley, Calif.
Corcoran Gallery of Art, Washington, D.C.
San Francisco Museum of Modern Art, San Francisco, Calif.
Nora Eccles Harrison Museum of Art, Logan, Utah
American Telephone and Telegraph, Boston, Mass.
Lytton Center of Visual Arts, Los Angeles, Calif.
Sheldon Memorial Art Gallery, Lincoln, Nebraska
di Rosa Preserve, Napa, Calif.

Select Personal Bibliography
Argus Courier, 1989, (interview)
Artforum, 1963; 1967; 1969 (review of work)
Art International, 1963; 1976 (review of work)
Art in America, 1977 (review of work)
Arts Magazine, 1968 (review of work)
Art News, 1976; 1977 (review of work)
Art Week, 1976; 1977; 1983; 1984; 1987 (review of work)
Braunstein Gallery, Fred Martin, 1985 (catalog)
North Bay Journal, 1984 (interview)
San Francisco Chronicle, 1970; 1983 (review of work)
San Francisco Museum of Modern Art, The Painting and Sculpture Collection, (book), 1985
San Jose Museum, Fred Martin, 1986 (catalog)
Sheldon Memorial Art Gallery, The American Painting Collection of the Gallery, 1989 (book)
Crown Publishing, NY, Collage and Assemblage, 1975, (book)
Thomas Albright, Art in the San Francisco Bay Area 1945-1980, 1985 (book)
The Press Democrat, 1992 (interview)
UOP Gallery, Carla Malone, 1991 (catalog)
Leonard Productions, The Art of Franklin Williams, 1992 (video art television)

Lectures
Crocker Art Museum; University of California, Davis; Whitney School of Art; Corcoran School of Art; New York University; New York Studio School; University of Nevada; Rohnert Park Chamber of Commerce; University of California, Santa Cruz; Chicago Art Institute; Charles Stewart Mott College; Eastern Michigan University; University of California, Irvine; College of Marin; Santa Rosa Junior College; Indian Valley College; Diablo Valley College; Sonoma State; San Jose State; Braunstein Gallery; University of Utah; Grent College of Higher Education, Newport, Wales; AICA New York Studio School; South Glamorgan Institute of Higher Education, Cardiff, Wales; Gwent College of Higher Education, Newport, Wales; Bristol Polytechnic, Bristol, England; School of Art & Design, Bristol, England; American River College; University of Pacific.

Research, Study and Travel
Dublin, Ireland; Edinburgh, Scotland; Florence, Rome, Siena, Venice, Italy; London, England; Mexico; New York; South West United States; Wales; Paris, France; Spain; Holland